WHY DON'T THEY TEACH THIS IN BIBLE SCHOOL?

31 Master Secrets Rarely Discovered

by
Sherman Owens

All Scripture quotations are taken from the *New King James Version* of the Bible.

ISBN 0-9642305-0-X

8200 Bee Ridge Rd.
Sarasota, Florida 34241

Published by Leadership Publishing

Printed in the United States of America.

CONTENTS

DEDICATION

To Mary, the sunshine of my life. My baby doll!

SPECIAL APPRECIATION

To Jesus, my Lord, who has given me life abundant.
Who has added years to my life,
and life to my years.

To my little girl, Marybeth, who typed, typed and
typed some more.
I love you.

To my son, Jimmy, who is on the mission field.
He fought the devil and won.
I'm so proud of him!

SPECIAL RECOGNITION

To my partners who believed in Jesus, wisdom and me. They made this first edition of "Why Don't They Teach This In Bible School?" possible. I ask you, Jesus, to multiply their seed back to them where they need it the most.

Jim Zirkle
Joseph and Ronni Federico
Brenda Howell
Elihu and Carolyn Brayboy
Frank and Lisa DiGiovanni
Kevin and Lenore Behrens
Ron and Pat Cherp
Maureen Morgan
Ronald Kutinsky
Bonnie Howell
Dave Webster
Ralph Hedrick
Marybeth Owens
Fran Rosenstein
Don and Heather Haus
Ernest and Eleanor Stockert
In Loving Memory of
Karra G. Haus
Eddie Longobardi
Don and Marty Blair
Roger and Laurie Hill
Linda Vanderherchen
Dennis McIntee
Darlene Rabelo
Todd Deroller

FOREWORD

Most men are very selfish with their success principles. They fear that others will take what they know and use it more productively. Not so with Pastor Sherman Owens, he is always seeking opportunity to enrich the lives of others.

In his book, "Why Don't They Teach This In Bible School?", he gives step by step encouragement and direction. Read it with pen and note paper, and you'll be blessed.

Dr. James Zirkle
President and Founder
Living Water Teaching

FOREWORD

Four words come to my heart as I consider the remarkable mantle on the life of Sherman Owens:

1. Integrity
2. Compassion
3. Brilliance
4. Tenacity

Those of us who have worked with him have seen relentless insistence on total integrity. If he says it, you can count on it. Character is a rare commodity these days.

Sherman Owens has never forgotten that the mercy and grace of God brought him to the heights he now enjoys. That explains why he takes time for little children as quickly as he reaches out to restore the crumbled dreams of hurting ministers. He never quits caring.

His mind is razor sharp and lightening fast. There is nothing sluggish about Sherman Owens. Nothing! He is perceptive, discerning and sees immediately what takes others a lifetime.

His loyalty toward his friends is legendary. He reaches, nourishes and waters consistently his garden of friendships. He has tenacity on holding on to relationships that matter.

That's why I listen to every single word that comes out of the heart and mouth of one of God's choicest and most unforgettable friends....Sherman Owens.

I could hardly wait for this book to be published. It will become a daily digest for many men of God.

Reading this book will be one of the best things you have ever done in your life.

Dr. Mike Murdock

WHY I WROTE THIS BOOK

At a seminar where I was teaching for Dr. Mike Murdock, he asked some ministers to share briefly on the "Five most important truths they learned since they have been in the ministry."

Those five truths have grown into Thirty One "Master Secrets" that have changed my life. I truly believe they will do the same for you.

Sherman Owens

MASTER SECRET 1

EVERYTHING RISES OR FALLS ON LEADERSHIP

"....set a man over the congregation, who may go out before them and go in before them, who may lead them out and bring them in, that the congregation of the Lord may not be like sheep which have no shepherd."

Numbers 27:16,17

I teach a leadership seminar entitled, "Things they don't teach in Seminary."

When I went into the ministry full-time, I thought all I needed were twelve red hot sermons. These I had, so I felt I was ready. I started Victory Christian Family Center (then Word of Faith) in the summer of 1980 in my home with two things: my "red hots" and vision. That will get you started, but I soon discovered there was something lacking called leadership. I was like a bull in a china closet. Soon after we got started, I called all my deacons together and asked them to please resign. I couldn't take it anymore! Before the meeting ended, we had all decided to give it one more try. I had made many mistakes, but I tried to learn from them.

I believe church growth is summed up in one word—leadership. Of course you must be filled with God's power, be in His will, and full of His Word, but without leadership skills, you won't get far. There are many successful men and women, who wouldn't know God if they bumped into Him, who have very successful businesses.

Why?

Leadership skills. There are many men and women of God who have the Spirit, but are not successful at all.

Why?

No leadership skills.

Why do churches grow to fifty but stay there? They might have one hundred visitors come through in a year, but they stay at fifty.

Why?

A lack of leadership skills!

Why do some grow to one hundred, two hundred, five hundred? Leadership skills!

Every Pastor *wants to* be successful, but it takes more than *want to*. We teach what we know, but we produce what we are. The first book of the Bible gives us this law:

"Everything produces according to their kind." (See Genesis 1:11, 12, 21, 24, 25, 26).

Most Pastors can preach, teach, marry, bury and raise money, but most haven't developed leadership skills. I believe that's why a lot of our Pentecostal churches are small. We have a lot of experience, but no expertise. I believe people want someone to take them somewhere, help them find God's will, and teach them how to live victoriously.

Jesus was a leader. When He left earth, He divided His ministry up and divided to each man as He willed, to train and equip His Body until He returns.

Time magazine asked the question a few months back, "Where are our leaders?"

I watched a group of experts discussing the 90's on television. They agreed we have all the resources to make this a great country, all that's missing is one thing—leaders! I believe that's true for the church. We have the Holy Spirit and the Word, all we need is leaders!

He Who Thinks He Is A Leader, But No One Is Following Him, Is Just Taking A Walk.

MASTER SECRET 2

RUN IN SUCH A WAY

"Do you not know that those who run in a race all run, but one receives the prize. Run in such a way that you may obtain it." I Corinthians 9:24

This verse must be stating that there is a right way and a wrong way to run. It is understood that Paul is talking about life, working, living and loving. Unlike a natural race, we all can win if we run in the right way! Paul said we are, "Competing for an imperishable crown." Do you see it? We are competing! Paul went on to say, "Because of that he did not run (compete) with uncertainty, he did not fight (compete) as one who beats the air." Paul's life had purpose, direction, and his punches had targets. Many of us are running hard all over the track! Many of us are busy punching, but we are simply shadow boxing. Ecclesiastes 10:10 paints us the picture clearly: ***"If the axe is dull and one does not sharpen the edge, then he must use more strength; but wisdom brings success."***

King Solomon is not trying to teach us how to be good lumberjacks! He is saying, "If you want to succeed, you must have a sharp axe." Many are chopping hard and long, but the tree is not coming down!

Why?

A dull axe! A wise man will stop and sharpen his axe. Listen, you are never wasting your time sharpening your axe. Wisdom brings success! Work hard, but also work smart!

Aren't you glad someone invented the chain saw?

"It Ain't The Things We Don't Know That Cause All The Trouble, It's The Things We Do Know That Ain't So." Artmas Ward

MASTER SECRET 3

A CHURCH HAS BOOKKEEPING

"Be diligent to know the state of your flocks, and attend to your herds." Proverbs 27:23

Most do not see the business or administrative side of the church. There is a part of the church that has to be run like a business. There is bookkeeping, budgets, payroll, administration, management, etc. The preaching and teaching are just the icing on the cake.

I remember Charles Capps made a statement in the 70's: "You don't substitute faith for good business principles, you don't substitute good business principles for faith. You use your faith in your good business."

There is a spiritual and practical side of ministry. The first deacons were elected and put in charge of the business of taking care of widows in Acts 6:3: ***"Therefore, brethren, seek out from among you seven men of good reputation, full of the Holy Spirit and wisdom whom we may appoint over this business."***

The reference to *business* in this scripture is the business of taking care of widows. The two sides of ministry are Mary and Martha. Mary sat at Jesus' feet being discipled, Martha served the food. Both were serving the Lord, both were needed. Jesus rebuked Martha, not for serving Him, but for putting the practical side first. Some want to be all Marys, some want to be all Marthas. We need both, but in order.

"Drive Thy Business, Or It Will Drive Thee."

Benjamin Franklin

MASTER SECRET 4

HAVE THE RIGHT PERSON IN THE RIGHT POSITION

"But now God has set the members, each one of them, in the body just as He pleased." I Corinthians 12:18

The eye cannot hear. The ear cannot see. The tongue cannot smell, but if each member is in his place the body will function properly. This might surprise you, but one of the greatest gifts of a leader is to have the ability to put the right person in the right position. One person out of place can weaken the entire organization. I heard an interview recently with a winning basketball coach. He was asked, "What is the secret of being a winning coach?" He said, "To have the ability to put the right player in the right position."

As I look back, I see a lot of my church problems stemmed from that inability. A study was done recently on successful pastors. Ninety-four percent (94%) of them had the ability to identify, recruit and train the right person for the right position. A personality profile is an excellent tool to help a leader do this. Just a few minutes, and you can pretty much tell if you have the right person for the position. It has been said that the success of any organization is attributable to three factors:

(1) Clear Direction

(2) Right Team Players

(3) Sound Finances

Success: (1) Clear Direction (2) Right Team Players (3) Sound Finances

MASTER SECRET 5

THE DIFFERENCE BETWEEN FAITHFULNESS AND LOYALTY

"And I thank Christ Jesus our Lord who has enabled me, because He counted me faithful, putting me into the ministry."

I Timothy 1:12

In the beginning I felt if someone showed up faithfully, on time, and could do the job, they qualified. I was wrong! Faithfulness refers to action. Loyalty refers to heart. Faithfulness is being on time, paying your tithes, working a full day. Loyalty is never talking about me behind my back. Loyalty is honoring the leader. Disloyalty cuts the bond that binds you together. You can train almost anyone to do a job, be on time, etc. But I question if you can train loyalty. Always hire loyalty and character, not talent!

Character is to be much more admired than talent. Do not hire people and make them good; hire good people to start with. Always ask yourself, "Can I trust this person?" Look for tell-tale signs. If they talk to you about someone else, they will talk to someone else about you. Faithfulness and loyalty are like a good composition, the words and the music go together.

Image is what others think you are. Character is what you really are. A fool has a character deficiency, not a mental deficiency.

Be What You Appear To Be.

MASTER SECRET 6

KEEP FOCUSED

"Then the Lord answered me and said: 'Write the vision, and make it plain on tablets, that he may run who reads it.'" Habakkuk 2:2

People only catch what has caught you. People do not follow vision, they only follow a man with a vision. They follow results! That is one of the reasons Satan sends tests, trials, temptations, and storms to break your focus. Every minute you are trying to put out fires in the church delays your dream from becoming a reality. My heart will not reach for what it cannot see. When you take your eye off the vision, that's broken focus and discouragement can set in. Proverbs 29:18 says, ***"Where there is no revelation, the people cast off restraint."***

I believe this can mean that unless someone has vision, the people will perish, because people follow a man with a vision! Purpose is permanent. Goals and vision can be temporary. Purpose never changes, goals can. My purpose is to:

(1) Exalt

(2) Equip

(3) Edify

(4) Evangelize

Exalt God, equip and edify the body, then evangelize the world. In that order! God has priority over all. We minister to the Lord of the work before we try to do the work of the Lord. The five-fold ministry was given to equip the church so it could evangelize the world. My purpose has never changed, but some of my goals have. Some have been reached; some I let die because they were borrowed, not birthed. They were hand made, not God sent. I borrowed the goal by saying, "Me too!"

God doesn't hand out "cookie cutter" dreams. Some will be similar, but no two are exactly alike. Establish your priorities, organize your journey and keep focused. Your vision will attract winners and whiners. Don't listen to the whiners. Whiners are little people who go places and "boo" things.

I've learned that "seeing is believing." Many don't believe it because they won't see it. See it, believe it, ask for it, go for it, possess it!

Seeing is believing! Abraham saw a country.....Jesus saw the cross, Paul saw his goal. James said, "You have not because you ask not."

It could be that we ask not because we see not! See not, believe not, ask not, have not. What do you think?

See It, Believe It, Say It, Seize It.

MASTER SECRET 7

POWER OF ASSOCIATION

"He who walks with wise men will be wise, But the companion of fools will be destroyed." Proverbs 13:20

Dr. Mike Murdock has taught me about the importance of relationships. One of the first things wisdom will do when it enters your heart is to disconnect you from the wrong people. In Proverbs 2:10-13 we read the following:

"When wisdom enters your heart, and Knowledge is pleasant to your soul, Discretion will preserve you; Understanding will keep you, To deliver you from the way of evil, From the man who speaks perverse things, From those who leave the paths of uprightness to walk in the ways of darkness."

As I look back on my life, every advancement I had was connected to a person. It has been said, "If people don't like you, they will try to hurt you if they can. If they can't hurt you, they won't help you. If they have to help you, they won't hope for you."

Dr. Mike Murdock says, "No relationship is neutral. It will either increase you or decrease you."

You will not advance without the help of people. Everything I know I learned from someone else! I use all my brains, and I will use yours too, if I can. I've learned that when God sends someone into your life that advances you, then you should feed off of them and feed them. Always feed the goose that lays the golden egg for you. The people around you will determine your level of success. I'm no better than my staff. You must come to realize that other people can help you do a better job than you could do alone.

"Few People Are Successful Unless A Lot Of People Want Them To Be." Andrew Carnegie

MASTER SECRET 8

YOU CAN'T FIX THEM ALL

"Then he threw down the pieces of silver at the temple and departed, and went and hanged himself."

Matthew 27:5

As a pastor, you want to help everyone that comes to you. In the beginning, when I couldn't help someone, I felt like I had failed. But I soon realized that I cannot fix everyone's problem. I heard a long time ago that 70% of the people who come to you for help are serious and wanting. They are serious and they want help, but you cannot help them.

Why?

They are not willing! The 30% you can help are also serious and wanting, but they are willing to listen and do.

Many who come are only wanting your ear, not your mouth. It is true that there are times when people just need someone to talk to. I'm not talking about that. I'm referring to those who have their minds made up before they come for counseling. I also discovered that there is a big difference between someone with a problem and someone who makes a problem big. With many, when you solve a problem for them, they find another one the next day. You should never solve a problem for someone, solve it with them. There is a big difference between someone with a big problem and someone who makes a problem big. With some people, their problem is not the problem, but problems are their problem. The turmoil is in the way they view the problems and react to them. It's not what happens to you, but what happens in you that counts.

A Lot Of Folks Are Willing To Die Instead Of Change.

MASTER SECRET 9

STAY FRESH

"But grow in the grace and knowledge of our Lord and Saviour Jesus Christ." II Peter 3:18

When I stop growing, I'm finished! The law of growth is the law of life. It's one thing to get to the top (I'm not there), but it's another thing to stay there! When you are leading people, you must stay fresh with your walk with God. Most ministries fail in their walk long before they fail in their work.

You must strive to grow positionally. It's been said, "Your job will be obsolete in 10 years." Charles Exley, C.E.O. of I.C.R. said, "I've been in business thirty-six years. I've learned a lot but most of it doesn't apply anymore."

They say that when trees stop growing, they die. In other words, when you are through improving, you are through! What I do for myself is more important than what others do for me. Growth is not doing the things you like to do, but doing the things you need to do when you need to do them. This concept is simple, but simple doesn't mean easy! The way to get more of God is to enlarge yourself. If you go to a waterfall with a cup, you come away with a cup of water. The problem is not the waterfall, but the size of your cup. When you enlarge your container, you enlarge your capacity to receive from God.

God only fills what He finds. Enjoy today, but live for tomorrow. You enlarge yourself by thinking, studying, reading, praying, asking, reaching, stretching and listening. Make decisions that benefit your future.

Play Now, Pay Later. Pay Now, Play Later.

MASTER SECRET 10

ACCEPT RESPONSIBILITY FOR THE GROWTH OF YOUR MINISTRY

"....and the Lord added to the church daily those who were being saved." Acts 2:47

Something is wrong if a child is ten years old and weighs ten pounds. Something is wrong with a church that is ten years old and has ten members. It's easy to blame the location, the people, the accommodations. Most pastors believe that they would pastor a larger church if they were somewhere else. But if you are not doing it where you are, you won't do it where you are not. Accept the responsibility for growth. If you want to know the temperature of a church, place the thermometer in the pastor's mouth! I believe that the key is to produce growth in the people and then they will produce growth in the church.

(1) Show the people

(2) Grow the people

(3) Go the people

No Excuses!

We Are Playing Follow The Leader.

MASTER SECRET 11

BE WILLING TO CHANGE

"But we all, with open face beholding as in a glass the glory of the Lord, are changed into the same image..."

II Corinthians 3:18

When you are through growing then you are through! Growing means one thing....change! Human beings resist change. It's so easy to get everything the way you like it, then coast. It's called the comfort zone. You need a comfort zone, but you work in a challenge zone. Most people choose to die rather than change. I heard this a long time ago: "When the pain of staying the same outweighs the pain of change, you will change."

When the advantages of change outweigh the disadvantages of change, then we will change. The experts say, "My job will be obsolete in ten years."

Clothes that are outdated are no longer used. Cars change, clothes change, buildings change. We need to also change our minds. They can become outdated. Look for new ideas and information. It's all around you. Ask someone who knows. It's not normal for a ten year old child to be sucking his thumb.

Don Shelby says, "When we tell ourselves 'I can never change' or 'That will never happen' we presume too much and believe too little."

One Of Life's Greatest Tragedies Is A Man Equipped For The Ocean, But He Is Rafting In A Millpond.

MASTER SECRET 12

LEARN FROM MY MISTAKES

"Now the Word of the Lord came to Jonah the second time." Jonah 3:1

The only value of a mistake is what you learn from it. Why make them if you don't learn from them? Golfers who consistently win all have one thing in common, they have the ability to recover from a bad lie. No one hits it perfectly every time. Many of my projects fail, but I never fail, because I am not a failure! There's a big difference between a man who says, "I have failed" and a man who says, "I am a failure."

Abraham Lincoln said, "Success is going from failure to future without losing your enthusiasm."

Ski instructors say, "If you are not falling, you are not learning!"

Failure is not making a mistake. It's making the same mistake continually. If you don't learn from past mistakes, there's a good chance you will repeat them. The best rodeo bronco rider gets thrown off every now and then, but he gets back up, dusts himself off, and climbs back on again. Failure is not in the falling. Failure is allowing yourself to stay down. The Bible starts off with a couple who missed it!

Climb On Again.

MASTER SECRET 13

LEARN TO TRAIN YOUR STAFF

"Then Jesus, going up to Jerusalem, took the twelve disciples aside....and said to them...." Matthew 20:17

No one comes fully equipped. If I do not train my staff, who will? The three growths of the church are:

(1) Grow Up

(2) Grow Together

(3) Grow Out

You are only as strong as your foundation. The stronger the foundation, the stronger the building. As a kid, I remember making sand castles at the beach. I discovered you can only pile sand as broad as your base. The higher you go, the broader the base. A church will never be greater than its leaders. It's those leaders around you who will determine your level of success. At my church, I have a special training session with my staff once a month, and I also send them to training seminars. We have a professional day, once a month where each staff member goes out into the business world, or maybe to another church, and spends the day with someone in his same area of ministry.

Leaders: Love everybody, but give yourself to your leaders! If you don't train them, somebody else will, but incorrectly.

Strive for unity and peace among your leaders. If the head is aching, the body hurts.

"When Elephants Fight, It Is The Grass That Suffers!" Kikuyu Proverb

MASTER SECRET 14

FORGIVE

"Then Jesus said, "Father forgive them, for they do not know what they do." Luke 23:34

Unforgiveness stops me cold! But forgiveness releases me from the bonds forged by someone else. Your vision, your anointing, and your mission will attract opposition. People will divide into two groups:

(1) The *bought* it group

(2) The *fought* it group

Some will feel an assignment from God to destroy you, and every minute you are defending your course, you are not advancing. Usually, the people who attack you are either jealous, uninformed, or both! When someone attacks me, I've learned not to pull out of gear. Don't get down on their level. Don't dirty yourself.

Dr. Lester Sumrall says, "Little people cause trouble." I've learned to pray for them. If I am right, all the demons of hell will not change what the angels say about me. If you have a problem with a brother, go to him, never at him. In II Timothy 4:10, Demas forsook Paul.

Paul said, "Lord, don't lay that to his account." Alexander the Coppersmith came at Paul, and Paul said, "May the Lord repay him for what he has done."

Paul forgave Alexander the Coppersmith, but there was a harvest for what he had done to Paul, unless he repented. Forgiveness is not a sign of weakness. You can forgive and still be strong. Do not become bitter!

Bitterness is worse than betrayal. Bitterness will lead to betrayal, because bitterness is an inside job which will manifest on the outside in the form of betrayal.

Forgive. Just Do It!

MASTER SECRET 15

PLAY TO WIN

"....Run in such a way that you may obtain it."
I Corinthians 9:24

Many play not to lose. Winning isn't number one, but it is important. Wanting to win isn't number one, but it is also important. The number one thing is the willingness to prepare to win. It's easy to have a burst of faith and energy in the beginning. Then, after things get going well, lay back and just maintain. Look at it this way, wanting to win is breakfast, the willingness to prepare to win is lunch, and winning is supper time!

It's Twice As Important To Finish A Job As To Start A Job.

MASTER SECRET 16

KEEP MY PANTS ON

"Flee also youthful lusts." II Timothy 2:22

Paul instructed Timothy to flee....That means if you have to flee from them, they are still after you. Just because you get older doesn't mean....(you finish it).

I don't need to tell you how this one has caused many good men to fall. My good friend, Dr. James Zirkle, says, "An 18 year old girl switching along in tight jeans looks as good to me today as when I was eighteen years old."

He has made some quality decisions to sleep in the right bed and drink out of the right bottle. Jim is successful because he is honest. A minister needs a good, strong relationship and fellowship with his or her mate, sexually! It could save the ministry!

I read a statement in "Ministries Today" that one of the world's outstanding Pastors, David Yonggi Cho made. This Pastor of the world's largest church said, "There are three areas where ministers fall to temptation: Money, Power and Women. I do not have a problem with being tempted by money. I have no problem with being tempted by power, but I do recognize in myself the possibility of being tempted by women, so I take steps to avoid being tempted. For example, when I travel I always go in the company of several elders; that way there is no time when I might find myself in a situation where temptation might take place."

Never forget that all great leaders have weaknesses. Dr. Lester Sumrall says, "All great men have feet of clay."

Dr. Cho is aware of his weaknesses; better yet, he is honest about his weaknesses. A minister can be very successful in his work of the Lord, while failing in his walk with the Lord. A minister fails in his private life long before he fails publicly. The Apostle Peter is an example of a frightening thing. Great leaders that hear from God also hear from Satan! On one page of your Bible in Matthew 16:13 Jesus asked, ***"Who do men say that I the son of man am?"***

In verse 16 Peter answered, ***"You are the Christ."***

Jesus answered Peter, ***"Flesh and blood has not revealed this to you, but my Father who is in heaven."***

Peter heard from God! On the next page of your Bible Peter rebuked Jesus for saying that he must go to Jerusalem and suffer and be killed. Jesus answered Peter's rebuke by saying, ***"Get behind me Satan! You are an offense to me for you are not mindful of the things of God, but the things of men."***

One minute Peter heard from God, the next minute Satan.

Look at Abraham. In Genesis 15 he heard from God, ***"You are my covenant man."***

The next day Abraham is jumping around in the tent with Haggar! Adam and Eve walked and talked with God, and the next minute they were hearing from the devil. Moses received the Ten Commandments directly from God, then he heard from the Devil and struck the rock. It robbed him from the land of Milk and Honey. Many leaders today don't get to taste the grapes, because they have fallen.

There can also be doors you open as a young man (or woman) that you have to work hard to close, such as pornography. What nags you, when you are young, will destroy you when you are old, if it is not taken care of.

I never put myself into the position where anything could happen. I never counsel women, my wife does that. She doesn't counsel men. Many are not in the ministry today because of something that started off innocently. I have a friend who's in heaven today because he wanted to help a hurting woman. He lost his ministry, his family for a season, and eventually his life. He was a good man, loved God, and one of the best Bible teachers I have ever heard. It's not worth it....keep your pants on!

"Drink Water From Your Own Cistern."
Proverbs 5:15

MASTER SECRET 17

THE POWER OF ACCOUNTABILITY

"How the mighty have fallen". II Samuel 1:17

The skirts are being lifted, everywhere you look, in the government, military, and Wall Street. The mighty are falling. It's one thing getting to the top, it's another to stay there. Ministers have been caught drinking out of the wrong bottle, sleeping in the wrong bed, and their hand in the wrong pocket. Many have fallen, and it's rocked the church. If you are a minister, this could be the most important Master Secret for you.

Some have left the church, never to return. If one falls, it hurts us all. The church has always had leadership problems. Jesus had one that sold Him, and one that denied Him.

Ministers who fall all have one thing in common:

(1) No daily prayer

(2) No daily Word

(3) Love of money or Love of power

(4) Lust

(5) No Accountability

(6) None of them believed it would happen to them

In I Corinthians, the tenth chapter, Paul speaks of our Fathers, and brothers, and sisters who went on before us. All were baptized into Moses, all ate the same spiritual food, all drank the same spiritual drink, but with most of them God was not pleased. Paul stated that they are our examples to the intent that we should not lust after evil things, as they also lusted. Then in verse twelve, Paul says, ***"Therefore let him who thinks he stands take heed lest he fall."***

I think I'm standing strong! So, I had better take heed lest I fall! Understand, when I look at this list of what fallen ministers have in common, anybody with a flesh and blood body can fall. If I am wise, I will take steps to avoid making the same mistakes they did, because I also do not believe it will happen to me. I make sure I am in the Word and prayer. I schedule it because you never find time for the Word and prayer. I am careful about the handling of money and power. I realize that my genes would react to pornography, just like the next man. I agree with my friend, Dr. James Zirkle, that an eighteen year old (or some forty eight year old) girl switching along in tight jeans looks as good to me today as she did when I was eighteen, so I've made some decisions not to lust. I have also made myself accountable. I believe one of the greatest needs of pastors today is to have someone they can be accountable to. Most pastors do not have a close friend, someone that believes in them and really cares; someone that can speak into their life. We need someone who understands we all have feet of clay. We need a man or woman of God we could go to and share our heart and not be betrayed, but really helped. I have such a friend. We made a Covenant Partner Agreement. Every time we meet we ask each other the following fifteen questions:

(1) Are you in prayer and the Word?

(2) Have you honored your vow to your wife?

(3) Are you providing spiritual leadership for your family?

(4) Are you in harmony with your spouse?

(5) Are you in conflict with anyone?
(6) Have you looked at any pornography?
(7) Have you stolen anything?
(8) Have you lied to anyone?
(9) Have you kept your commitments?
(10) Are you taking care of your body?
(11) What are you doing to show love and appreciation to those who work for you?
(12) Are you in your assignment?
(13) What are you struggling with now?
(14) How can I help you in your weakest area?
(15) Have you been completely honest with me?

I do not want to let God, my family, or my friend down. I believe there is power in being accountable. If you knew these questions would be asked of you every month by someone you loved and admired, I believe it could help you say, "No."

I believe for God to put a real friend into your life.

"As Iron Sharpens Iron So A Man Sharpens The Countenance Of His Friend."
Proverbs 27:17

MASTER SECRET 18

BE GRATEFUL

"Giving thanks always for all things to God the Father in the name of our Lord Jesus Christ." Ephesians 5:20

What you are grateful and thankful for will always increase in your life.

Practice gratefulness. Be thankful for little things. Don't take things for granted.

Paul said in I Corinthians 4:7: ***"What do you have that you did not receive?"***

Gratefulness could be the healthiest of all emotions. Revenge could be the worst. Where would you be without God? Ungratefulness means that we do not understand life. What you put in, you get out. The instant you were born, you owed someone nine months room and board. Be grateful!

It has been aptly stated, "If you have nothing to be thankful for, make up your mind that there is something wrong with you."

A Grateful Mind Is A Great Mind.

MASTER SECRET 19

DON'T PREACH TO EMPTY CHAIRS

"For God is not unjust to forget your work and labor of love...." Hebrews 6:10

It's easy for a pastor to take out his frustrations on the faithful. Some don't support the meeting you've worked so hard on, and you end up taking it out on the ones who do. Remember, if it weren't for the ones who were there, you could be back on the time clock again.

Once, we had ordered a large order of chairs and the trucker was unloading them. He heard we were a new church, so he said to me, "You must be telling these folks what they want to hear."

I answered, "No, I'm telling them what they need to hear in a way they want to hear it."

We pastors need to love, build and train what we get, then God will give us more. Don't preach to empty chairs, they are not there!

"A Few Fish Can Turn Into A Multitude, If They Are Handled Right." Sherman Owens

MASTER SECRET 20

WORK HARD

"A little sleep, a little slumber, a little folding of the hands to sleep, so shall your poverty come on you like a robber...."
Proverbs 6:10-11

Wisdom brings success, and wisdom is the correct application of knowledge, so success is working hard and smart.

Ecclesiastes 10:10 says, ***"If your axe is dull more strength is required, but wisdom brings success."***

A wise man will stop and sharpen his axe. He will get much more done with less energy. A study said, "Simply working hard puts you into the top 50% of the work force."

It's one thing gathering all the principles for success, but none of them will work unless you do them. It has been said, "Success is dressed in overalls."

God gives you the shovel, you dig. Robert Frost said, "The world is filled with willing people; some willing to work, the rest willing to let them."

Did you ever notice that when you run into a man with real enthusiasm for hard work, he turns out to be your boss? Most footprints on the sands of time were left by work shoes.

It has been said, "There are two ways to the top of an oak tree, sit on an acorn, or climb!"

Failing is not in falling, it's doing nothing. A great occasion will require preparation. Find your tree, sharpen your ax, then go to work!

"The Only Place That Success Comes Before Work Is In The Dictionary." Vidal Sassoon

MASTER SECRET 21

THE POWER OF ORDER

"Let all things be done decently and in order."
I Corinthians 14:40

Recently I spoke with a young man who has the call of God on his life. He is doing well, but it was brought to my attention that he kept his room in a mess. I normally would never say anything about something like this, but the door was open. So, I shared with him how something that little, no matter how unspiritual it might seem, could keep him from the ministry. I told him, "That mess will not just stay in your room, it will manifest in all parts of your life; there is power in order!"

I believe that a man that has no taste for order will often be wrong in his judgment.

It has been said, "Organizing is what you do before you do something, so that when you do it, it's not all mixed up."

When you are organized, you have a special power. You walk with a clear, sure sense of purpose; your priorities are clear. Things fall into place.

Four questions to ask before you start your project:

(1) What to?

(2) Why to?

(3) How to?

(4) When to?

Some let God tell them what and why, then they let the devil tell them how and when.

What deals with mission.

Why deals with motive.

How deals with vision.

When deals with timing.

Your mission is your purpose. That never changes! Why are you on this planet? What's your calling? Stop now and answer that question. Now!

Why are you doing what you are doing? Why do you want the largest church in town?

Why do you want a TV ministry? Answer that question. Now!

What's your vision for your mission? How are you going to accomplish your mission? Pastor, evangelize, teach? Help someone else? Answer it!

When are you going to start? Until you answer the last question, the rest doesn't matter!

What Do I Want? Am I Willing To Pay The Price? When Will I Start Paying The Price?

MASTER SECRET 22

THINK!

"Finally Brethren, whatever things are true, noble, just, pure, lovely, good report, virtue, praiseworthy, think on these things." Philippians 4:8

Thinking is a lost art. Take a minute. Stop and think. Don't let anger or pressure interfere with your thinking; the answer might be there. Draw it out. There is no guarantee that thinking big will produce big results, but thinking little will produce little results!

It has been said, "The greatest threat....if doers learned to think and thinkers learned to do."

If you don't think for yourself, someone will do it for you! Do you want that?

There are two kinds of people:

(1) Those who stop to think

(2) Those who stop thinking

"If You Don't Know What You Want To Achieve, Then Any Sort Of Thinking Will Do."
Dr. Eric Bienstock

MASTER SECRET 23

DON'T GET TOO SMART

"Let him who thinks he stands take heed lest he fall."
I Corinthians 10:12

We have all seen it, or felt it. Ministers with the big head. I understand that our members tell us every week how wonderful we are and how well we preach. The problem is, we start believing it. Now, we should feel good about ourselves, but without God we are nothing! When we start believing we are God's special elect, that the people can't get along without us, we are in for a fall. A *Wall Street Journal* article told why smart people do dumb things. The story told of a young man who was President of Fox Network. He had hired a young man to strip as he was giving a speech on censorship. He misjudged his peers' morals and was fired! This management consultant studied a wide assortment of stupid decisions made by people with IQs off the chart. Here's what he found:

(1) **Arrogance:** Smart guys get used to knowing more than anybody else. It's a short step from knowing more, to thinking you know everything.

(2) **Isolation**: Smart people tend to isolate themselves. They surround themselves with other smart people. That's good, but feedback is essential. They become impatient with anyone slower than themselves....hard to listen. When Harry Truman became President, Sam Rayburn gave him some fatherly advice, "From here on out you're going to have lots of people around you.

They'll try to put a wall around you and cut you off from any ideas but theirs. They'll tell you what a great man you are Harry, but you and I both know you ain't."

(3) **Recklessness:** Their attitude is, "Now for my next trick." They become risk junkies. Gary Hart said, "Catch me if you can!" They did!

Many super-brains cannot grasp simple facts. "Brilliant in one area is no guarantee of success in another." Successful people listen and think. Smart people refuse to take themselves too seriously. They know their own limits.

A very experienced old teacher once said, "Students that go on to achieve the most are almost never the top students."

Keep Yourself Little In Your Own Eyes So God Can Be Big.

MASTER SECRET 24

THE BETTER THE PLAYER, THE HIGHER THE SCORE

"Seek out from among you seven men of good reputation, full of the Holy Spirit, and wisdom...." Acts 6:3

Many times in the ministry we hire what is readily available or what we feel we can afford. We overlook the best qualified, because we feel they would have to step down to come into the ministry. The answer is that when you cannot afford to hire the best, hire the young that want to be the best. Hire hearts, not heads. Hire character, not talent. Hire team players, not loners. Don't hire talented people and try to make them good, hire good people to start with. You can train a good person to do almost anything. Milton Olson, a Naturalist, did a study on Geese. We can learn a lot from the Geese. Let me share what scientists have discovered:

(1) As each bird flaps its wings, it creates an up-lift for the bird following. By flying in a "V" formation, the whole flock adds 71% greater flying range than if the bird flew alone.

Lesson: People who share a common direction and sense of community can get where they are going quicker and easier, because they are traveling on the thrust of one another.

(2) Whenever a goose falls out of formation, it suddenly feels the drag and resistance of trying to fly alone, and quickly gets back into formation to take advantage of the lifting power of the bird immediately in front.

Lesson: If we have as much sense as geese, we will stay in formation with those who are headed where we want to go, and we will be willing to accept their help as well as give ours to others.

(3) When the lead goose gets tired, it rotates back into formation, and another goose flies at the point position.

Lesson: It pays to take turns doing the hard tasks and sharing leadership. With people, as with geese, we are interdependent on each other.

(4) The geese in formation honk from behind to encourage those up front to keep up their speed.

Lesson: We need to make sure that our honking from behind is encouraging.

(5) When a goose gets sick or wounded or is shot down, two geese drop out of formation and follow it down to help and protect it. They stay with it until it is able to fly again or dies. Then they launch out on their own with another formation, or catch up with their flock.

Lesson: If we have as much sense as geese, we too will stand by each other in difficult times, as well as when we are strong.

If the pastors can assemble men and women to work together like the geese, the sky is the limit!

The Better The Players, The Higher The Score.

MASTER SECRET 25

BELIEVE YOU CAN, AND THE HOW TO WILL SHOW UP

and Jesus said to them, "If you can believe, all things are possible to him who believes." Mark 9:23

I shared earlier that we started Victory Christian Family Center with my twelve Red Hots and Vision. We met in a recreational center Sunday afternoons at two p.m.; that was the only time we could get in. We started in August; it gets hot in Florida in August without air conditioning. All we had were big fans that blew the hot air around and around. We also were directly under the landing zone next to the airport. I would have to stop preaching as the jets flew over; it would give me time to dry off. We grew, and from there we moved to a theater. Then, as we continued to grow, we moved to a former gay bar. We cleaned it out, and grew from there to a business complex. The ministry expanded during this time, so we began to look for land, and found nine acres on a main boulevard. We drew our building plans, got a lawyer, and went before the County Commission for approval at the meeting. The place was packed. When our turn came up, one of the Commissioners said, "Is there anyone here tonight that is in opposition to this building project?" Everyone in the room stood up. You talk about rejection jumping on you! Ninety percent (90%) of the neighborhood came out to say, "NO church in our neighborhood!"

We were turned down, so it was back to the drawing board. We found another lawyer to present our plan to the Board. We then found five acres of land, went into the neighborhood and surveyed each home. We told them who we were, what we were doing there, and asked if they would mind if we built a church. We received eighty plus signatures on a petition stating that they would like this church in their neighborhood. All but three signed the petition. We then went back to the Commissioners with our petition.

"Anyone here tonight that is in opposition to this church project?"

One lady stood up and said she bred horses, and a church was incompatible with her business. One old man that lived across from our land said that he didn't want a church across from him. We told the Commissioners we would put up a fence so the horses wouldn't be bothered with us while they did their breeding. We then brought in a horse and breeding expert who testified the church would in no way bother the horses. The old man moved away during the proceedings, but they turned us down!

Back to the drawing board; new lawyer, new plans. This time we found twelve acres next to the interstate. Back to the Commissioners. We got a prayer group together at the church to pray while the meeting was going on. We got to the Courthouse; again, a full house.

"Oh my God, not again!"

"Anyone here...." again, the whole house stood up, " We are not against churches, but our roads won't take the traffic."

The Commissioner said, "Disapproved, next case."

I went back to the church, talking all the way to God. "God, I've got this prayer group to face; did I miss it?"

God simply said, "No, they missed it."

I walked in, and they were all praying and standing in a circle praising God. I said, "I'm going to find out who really understands faith here; you are praying and praising God, but will you praise God after I tell you the news?"

Smiling, I said, "They turned us down!"

Their faces were blank. One started shouting, "Praise God, He is faithful...., the Word is working...." Then another and another. It was short, but we had a praise party. I told the people, "I will not quit. God has called me to Sarasota, Florida. The devil is a liar, and God has something bigger and better!"

They say three strikes and you are out; that's a lie! You keep swinging until you hit the ball, but then you have to run the bases. By the way, all this took about two to three years.

Back to the drawing board; new lawyer, and looking for land. Guess what we found? Fifty one acres, two miles off the interstate, for $6,500 an acre! We signed the contract, got our lawyer, and showed up for our meeting. The room was again full...."God help me!" "Anyone here tonight...."

No one stood up. He stamped our papers "APPROVED". It took less than five minutes. We left shouting and praising God. We are now in a beautiful complex, a Garden Mall and Learning Center. Now the brown paper bag miracle. Are you ready? Steadfastness pays off! When we built our Garden Mall, we were about $400,000 short, so we cut off the sanctuary and used what was to be the Children's Church. It would seat about 600 people. We moved in. The church was going great, growing. Our school was started, and it was growing. Praise God, the storms are over! Little did I realize our biggest attack was on the way. Your anointing will attract attack!

Mike Murdock has said that Satan will attack you the greatest right before a promotion—he is right! When we moved in our new Garden and Learning Center I put up two little signs that said, "New Sanctuary" which led out to where our new sanctuary was to be. We started believing for God to do it somehow. Then it hit! One of our leaders had an affair with another member—it hurt. Some people will not stay with you when the attack comes; they feel a church shouldn't have problems. But remember, a church has problems because people have problems, and people come to church. A year later one of my staff members turned on me, little by little, saying little things to other people, disloyal. I had to let him go. After he was released, we discovered he had been stealing from the church. I met with him, he confessed, and said he couldn't believe he had been so deceived and asked for me to please forgive him. But a member of his family felt God had anointed them to expose me. Lies were spread, and, like always, a few believed them and left without checking anything out. It hurt. Then the final wave hit. A year later, another staff member was found in a girly bar dancing with topless women. He confessed to me, and said if I wanted to let him go, he would understand. I said no, I will work with you, if you are willing; he agreed. I got him an outside counselor, who was trained in this kind of situation, plus our staff counselor worked with him. After six months both counselors reported that he was not responsive. I asked him to get up before the leadership and repent. He wouldn't do it! I let him go, and he led a vicious attack against me. He wrote a letter to most of the church members, plus many of the youth and to several speakers we had speak at our church. He threatened to sue if I didn't give him $12,000. I didn't respond. If he sued, so be it.

He wrote a second letter, and I got the church together and answered each of his charges. They said they didn't need to hear it because they believed in me. But, like always, a few would rather believe a lie. I've found in most cases it justifies their own sin. He finally decided not to sue. The organization which had ordained him found out and pulled his ordination papers. During all this attack we built an entrance on our Learning Center. But we still needed a sanctuary, and our school needed even more class rooms. We had lost about 150 people, but 500 stayed! I began to make the statement, "The money for our new sanctuary is coming in, even if God has to bring it in a brown paper bag in a dog's mouth!" Several months later, I felt inside me, "It's time." I got our leadership together and told them it's time. I'm believing for the seed of our new sanctuary to be birthed in you tonight; I see it! I've preached in it, now it's time to build it even if God has to bring it in a brown paper bag in a dog's mouth. I asked them to each sow a $12.00 seed to start the new sanctuary fund. The Sunday before this, Mike Murdock spoke in our church, and said that God was dealing with someone in the church to give a large gift to Victory. The next Sunday a couple asked if we could get together soon. We met with them the next week, and they told us God had been dealing with them for sometime. In my prayer time I had been calling in hundred thousand dollar checks for our new sanctuary and class rooms. They handed me a check that night for $20,000 and said, "we will give the church a $20,000 check each month until $400,000 comes in!" If that's not a brown paper bag miracle, then I don't know what is! My wife began to cry. I was praising God, and I really believe I saw a dog in a vision wag his tail! As I write this, we are beginning to build our new sanctuary. It will take more than $400,000, but I'm looking down the road, and any day now I will see another dog with a brown paper bag in his mouth!

"Come Here Boy"

MASTER SECRET 26

YOU ARE NOT IN CHARGE

"God is not mocked; for whatever a man sows, that he will also reap." Galatians 6:7

Hold on to your hat! I have some frightening news for you....You are not in control of your life! I know that's hard to accept. Several years ago I would have rebelled against such a statement, but it's a fact, you are not in charge. God's universal laws and principles are, but you are in control of your own decisions. This could be the greatest power God has given us. We make decisions everyday to be bitter or better, give up or get up, Heaven or Hell....it's all our decision. You cannot change the consequences of your choices. Every decision is a seed, and the harvest from your decisions are governed by God's laws. From your decision on, you are not in control. The law you set in motion is: "Whether you like it or not"! The law says, "What will be."

Why are you married to that man or woman today? Because you married him yesterday.

Why are you overweight? Because you ate it yesterday.

Why can't you get a better job? Because you quit school yesterday.

Why do you have a house full of children? Because you planted the seed yesterday.

Everything you are or become, you grew into. Everything you have or don't have, you sowed for. See, you are not in control, your seed is! The only way you can say what will be is by sowing the right seed. When you sow, you are saying, "This is what I want."

From there on, the harvest is in the hands of God's laws. You can pray, grunt, cry, beg, plead, promise, give, sacrifice, but, as long as that law is in motion, nothing will change. God's laws are absolute. Changing God's laws in your life are like trying to change gravity; you don't decide which way you go when you decide to jump, you go down.

Why?

The law is in control. I see people all the time who are not happy. They really don't like their life. If they were in control it would be different. They would change, but they don't know how. In Galatians 6:7 we read the following: ***"God is not mocked; for whatever a man sows, that he will also reap."***

How can you mock God? By believing you can over-ride God's law of sowing and reaping. When you believe you can sow bad and not reap bad, you are making fun of God's law. When you pick up one end of the stick, you also pick up the other end. Christians are good at making wrong decisions, using bad judgment, exercising bad management, and then blaming their harvest on "God's will", or they say, "God is testing me." No, your bad decision planted your harvest. Many will also say, "Why me God?" Why not you, you planted it! Understand, the Word is working in you. In Isaiah 55:11 God said His Word would not return to Him void, ***"It shall accomplish what I please."***

God's word always works. God says, "If you do this, this will happen and if you don't do this, this will happen."

You can't change that. Someone said, "The Word doesn't work for me." Yes, it does! "Then why am I broke, sick and sad?" Because the Word is working in you. Please understand, God is not making you sick, broke and sad. God wants His children to prosper and be in health like He stated in III John 2. It's our decision; we decide to apply His principles or not. Have you ever heard someone say, "God is in control?" Well if He is, He's got this world in a mess. I believe you would agree things could be better. It's true God's laws are in control, but we activate them.

What you are going to be tomorrow, you are becoming today. The seed you are sowing today, you will harvest tomorrow. You are living yesterday's decisions today. You can't get to harvest time and say, "I change my mind." Those who do not realize how their yesterday has affected their today will never understand how their today will affect their tomorrow. That's why there is no quick fix, because nothing takes the place of the seasons. There is a time for planting, watering and weeding. In Galatians 6:9 it says, ***"In due season we shall reap if we do not lose heart."***

You can want to do the right thing, you can even want to do it for the right reason. It can even be holy, righteous, or a command from God, but if you do not apply the right principles, you will hit a wall every time.

"And Let Us Not Grow Weary While Doing Good, For In Due Season We Shall Reap, If We Do Not Lose Heart."   Galatians 6:9

MASTER SECRET 27

THE LAW OF THE FARM

"While the earth remains, seed time and harvest....shall not cease." Genesis 8:22

What if we could understand how the Kingdom of God works. Do you think it would help us improve our life? Listen to what Jesus said in Mark 4:26, ***"The Kingdom of God is as if a man should scatter seed on the ground."***

Wow! Did you hear what Jesus said? ***"The Kingdom of God is...."***

Jesus is painting a picture for us about how His Kingdom works. In verse 30 Jesus said, ***"To what shall we liken the Kingdom of God or what parable shall we picture it. It is like a mustard seed when it is sown on the ground...."***

Again, Jesus is telling us Kingdom principles. You could say God's Kingdom is ruled by the Law of the Farm. The Law of the Farm is the mystery of life. Again, in Mark 4:11 Jesus said, ***"To you it has been given to know the mystery of the Kingdom of God."***

When Jesus said these incredible things, He had just finished teaching about the parable of the sower. In Mark 4:13-20 we read the following:

"And He said to them, 'Do you not understand this parable? How then will you understand all the parables? The sower sows the Word. And these are the ones by the wayside where the word is sown. When they hear, Satan comes immediately and takes away the word that was

sown in their hearts. These likewise are the ones sown on stony ground who, when they hear the word, immediately receive it with gladness; and they have no root in themselves, and so endure only for a time. Afterward, when tribulation or persecution arises for the word's sake, immediately they stumble. Now these are the ones sown among thorns; they are the ones who hear the word, and the cares of this world, the deceitfulness of riches, and the desires for other things, entering in choke the word, and it becomes unfruitful. But these are the ones sown on good ground, those who hear the word, accept it, and bear fruit: some thirty fold, some sixty, and some a hundred.'"

Notice Jesus mentions four different kinds of people. There are only four different kinds of people in the world:

(1) Wayside people = no growth

(2) Stony people = shallow growth

(3) Thorny people = stunted growth

(4) Good people = good growth

Within the Fourth group there are three levels:

30, 60 and 100

The first man is the indifferent; he doesn't care about the things of God, he is on the outside. The other three are on the inside. The second man is the shallow. He hears the Word, but he doesn't hang around long enough for it to take root. A little heat comes his way, and he is up and out. The third man is also on the inside. He hears the Word, but he is cluttered with the things of the world, and they choke the Word. The fourth man is the responsive one. He hears, receives, waters, weeds and reaps a harvest. It's the Law of the Farm!

With the first man the Word goes on, but not in. With the second man the Word goes on and in, but not down.

With the third man the Word goes on, in, down, but not up. Lastly, with the fourth man the Word goes on, in, down, and up! There is no fruit until it comes up!

Notice how none of the men were in control of his life, the Word is. God's Law of the Farm is in control. Remember, I said it takes time. In Mark 4:28-29 we read the following:

"For the earth yields crops by itself: first the blade, then the head, after that the full grain in the head. But when the grain ripens, immediately he puts in the sickle, because the harvest has come."

See the law of progression? God wants to put His seed in you.

Why?

Because you are His garden. In Proverbs 4:20-23 we read the following:

"My son, give attention to my words; incline your ear to my sayings. Do not let them depart from your eyes; keep them in the midst of your heart; For they are life to those who find them, and health to all their flesh. Keep your heart with all diligence, for out of it spring the issues of life."

For out of the heart spring the issues of life, or, you could say, the principles of life. In Isaiah 58:11 it says, *"You shall be like a watered garden."*

Gardens need tender care. We cannot put our garden (life) on automatic, and somehow expect the quality of life which comes from careful, consistent nurturing. Jesus said in John 10:10, *"I have come to give you life and give it to you abundantly."*

God's Word (seed) planted in your heart will bring forth life. We cannot toss out a few seeds, then go ahead and do whatever we want, and expect to come back and find a beautiful garden. If there is no gardener, there is no garden! You are the gardener of your life. God gives you the seed—His Word, and the hoe—the Holy Spirit, but He expects us to dig, plant, and nurture the seed. Things will grow without care, but what will be the outcome? WEEDS! If you understand this parable, you will understand life. Parables are all about life.

Be An On, In, Down, And Up Christian.

MASTER SECRET 28

THE SECRETS OF WISDOM

"Wisdom is the principle thing. Therefore get wisdom, and in all your getting get understanding. Exalt her and she will promote you." Proverbs 4:7-8

You are not in control, God's laws are, and so are His principles. Secrets of wisdom: If God's laws, principles, wisdom and Word are in control, we had better make a decision to get as much planted in us as we can. Listen to Job 11:6 ***"That He would show you the secrets of wisdom for they would double your prudence."***

My dictionary says the word prudence is to "Be careful to avoid errors and follow the most skillful and profitable course."

You might say prudence is how you apply wisdom. What if you had double the ability to avoid errors and follow the most skillful and profitable course? Would your life bring forth good things? Certainly!

Prudence also means calculation, canniness, discretion, forethought, observance, insight, discernment and judgment. What if you had double the ability of calculation, canniness, discretion, forethought, observance, insight, discernment and judgment? Would you prosper?

It's all found in the secrets of wisdom and God's principles. With most, it's still a secret. You can white knuckle it through life, swim upstream and grit your teeth; or you can sharpen your axe with God's Word. It makes life so much easier.

"Happy Is The Man Who Finds Wisdom. For Her Proceeds Are Better Than The Profits Of Silver, And Her Gain Than Fine Gold."
Proverbs 3:13,14

MASTER SECRET 29

THE FORCE OF PASSION

"Zeal for your house has eaten me up." Psalm 69:9

What I share with you now could be the single greatest ingredient for achievement. This could be the most overlooked master secret. Without this, all the wisdom will not help you, even vision will not help, your faith will not work. This is one thing I would give you if I could—

PASSION!

As I look at our great men of God, I see one thing common in all of them - Passion!

Mike Murdock says, "I have a craving for wisdom."

Do you know why he has so much wisdom? It's simple, he has passion for it. Wisdom is available to everyone, but not many have it.

Why?

They don't go after it. Wisdom is only found by passionate people, hungry people. In Proverbs 1:20-23 we read the following:

"Wisdom calls aloud outside; she raises her voice in the open squares. She cries out in the chief concourses, at the openings of the gates in the city she speaks her words: How long, you simple ones, will you love simplicity? For scorners delight in their scorning, And fools hate knowledge. Turn at my rebuke; surely I will pour out my spirit on you; I will make my words known to you."

Notice wisdom is everywhere crying out, but many refuse it. There will come a time in everyone's life when he or she will call on wisdom, but she will laugh at their calamity.

Why?

Because they didn't choose the fear of the Lord. Remember, you are only in control of your decisions. Wisdom is called "she." If you mistreat a woman, she will not be there when you need her. In your day of trouble she will not answer. In Proverbs, the second chapter, God tells us how to find wisdom. Proverbs 2:1-6 states:

"My son, if you receive my words, and treasure my commands within you, So that you incline your ear to wisdom, and apply your heart to understanding; Yes, if you cry out for discernment, and lift up your voice for understanding, If you seek her as silver, and search for her as for hidden treasures; Then you will understand the fear of the Lord, and find the knowledge of God, For the Lord gives wisdom; from His mouth come knowledge and understanding;"

Notice two things:

(1) Wisdom must be a treasure to you (verse one).

(2) You must go after her with a passion (that's how you got your mate).

Look at the words *incline, apply, cry out, lift up, seek* and *search.* These are all action words, all passionate words. Look at the results in Proverbs 2:10-12:

"When wisdom enters your heart, and knowledge is pleasant to your soul, Discretion will preserve you; understanding will keep you, To deliver you from the way of evil, from the man who speaks perverse things,"

When you read the Word of God, the way a hungry man reads a cook book, you will find wisdom. Wisdom is the reward of passion and wisdom brings success. The principles of wisdom are for assisting you to accomplish your purpose.

Look at men like Dr. Lester Sumrall, eighty-two years of age at the time of this writing. You can't keep up with him! Books are filled with his accomplishments and adventures. How does he do it? One word—Passion!

Look at Dr. James Zirkle. It's said he knows more about missions than any man living.

Why? Passion!

I believe if you look at all of our great men and women of God you will find passion. Sure they have vision, but you can have fizzled vision. But with passion, it sizzles. It's the ingredient that gives you the energy to reach, seek, search, go.... As a rule, passion is something you cannot hide. The most successful men in life have the best information, but to have it, you must go after it. It doesn't come to you. Once you have that information, things unnoticed come to light. You can now see opportunities clearly; they were there all the time, but unnoticed.

John Wesley traveled 250,000 miles on horseback, averaging twenty miles a day for forty years, preached 40,000 sermons, produced 400 books, knew ten languages, and at the age of eighty-three was annoyed that he couldn't write more than fifteen hours a day without hurting his eyes. At eighty-six he was ashamed that he could not preach more than twice a day. He complained in his diary that there was an increasing tendency to lie in bed until 5:30 in the morning. One word describes John Wesley—Passion!

The great missionary, Dr. Livingston, traveled 11,000 miles through the darkest jungle in Africa to spread the Word. Something drove him; he had unbelievable hardships, danger, wild beasts and disease. He was nearly killed by hostile tribes, robbed, beaten and left for dead by his own guides. On May 1, 1893, Dr. Livingston was found dead in a crude hut deep in the jungle on his knees in a position of prayer. One word describes Dr. Livingston—Passion!

Every great achievement is the story of a flaming heart.

People will travel for hours, sit for hours, and spend money to listen to someone with fire in his soul. We admire them, respect them, and wonder at them. A man with passion stands out from the crowd.

When the early church was filled with the Holy Spirit, they became street preachers. Peter stood and preached, and they were awe struck. Jesus sat down and made a whip to drive the hypocrites out of the temple.

Why? Passion!

David danced, Elijah called fire down from heaven and cut off four hundred and fifty false prophets heads. Noah built an ark, Samson pushed down the pillars of the temple and killed over three thousand heathens. John the Baptist lived in the desert and told the king he was going to hell. The Shunammite woman caught hold of Elisha's feet, and wouldn't let go until she got her miracle. Blind Bartimaeus wouldn't stop crying out for mercy. A man in the New Testament, with his four friends, tore a hole in the church roof to get to Jesus. The woman with the issue of blood pressed through that crowd to get to Jesus.

Who are these heroes of faith? Just average people with one special ingredient—Passion!

Passion must have the anointing of God. If not, you could have a Jim Jones or a Hitler. Fire in the fireplace is wonderful, but fire outside the fireplace is dangerous and destructive. Satan can pervert passion. Perverted passion is lust. Lust is of the flesh, passion is of the soul. God cannot anoint lust. Passion must be bridled, it must have the reigns of God's Word, or it will do much damage. I like a man with an opinion. A man without an opinion is dead. In I Kings 18:21 we read the following, ***"Why do you hesitate believing two opinions? If the Lord is God, follow Him, but if Baal, then follow him."***

Passion can get you into trouble and keep you out of trouble. If you have a passion for God, you can say, "No" to temptation. You will sleep in the right bed, and drink out of the right bottle. We know how to shout in the church; we need to know how to shout in the streets and on the roof tops. We have been quiet long enough.

Could the second greatest force be compassion?

It's Said That Eugene Ormandy Dislocated His Shoulder While Leading The Philadelphia Orchestra. I Wonder How Many Christians, Including Myself, Have Dislocated Anything Serving God?

MASTER SECRET 30

BE YOURSELF

"I will praise you, for I am fearfully and wonderfully made." Psalm 139:14

In the beginning, you tend to mimic your peers in the ministry. You admire them so much, but, if it's not you, it won't work. God doesn't hand out cookie cutter ministries. There are no two alike. You can believe alike and have similar visions, but there is only one you. Be all you can be, but be you! The privilege of life is to be you.

No one can do what you do. No one has your talent, your gifts, your personality; you are one of a kind. There are no carbon copies in God's creation. Don't mimic somebody else's successes. Success for me is seeing my red headed wife make notes when I teach, and my children fulfilled and serving the Lord. Don't set goals to impress someone else.

What's big in you?

God Doesn't Hand Out Cookie Cutter Ministries.

MASTER SECRET 31

MY STEPS TO CHANGE

"But we all, with unveiled face beholding as in a mirror the glory of the Lord, are being changed into the same image...." II Corinthians 3:18

I was raised in a little place called Samoset, Florida. There were a lot of good people that lived in Samoset, but it was a rough community, a place the world calls the wrong side of the tracks. I lived in a postage stamp world, never really believing or seeing myself breaking out into anything better. Back then, we didn't know what the word "dysfunctional" meant, but believe me we were a dysfunctional family. Understand, my problem wasn't that I was raised in Samoset; my problem was that Samoset was raised in me. I grew up in Samoset and Samoset grew up in me. Environment has an incredible power to influence your life, mold you, and it's not easy to get that junk out of you. If the problem was just the environment, we could just relocate everybody and they would be okay, but it's the environment that gets in you that hurts. All the water in the world won't sink your boat if it doesn't get in it. I felt inferior, I believed I was. I found out later that you will not consistently function in a manner that you do not believe about yourself. Before you can, you must believe that you can. Before you can do, you must be. I failed three grades before the Ninth grade. I honestly believe if you were to put my brain in a Blue Jay, it would fly backwards! I went in the army as a private, and three years later I came out a private. Soon after, I met my red-head and was married. Ten years later, I finally hit bottom. I was a drunk, gambler, and about to lose my job and home. I found myself, early one morning, waking up with the sun shining in my eyes. I had gotten drunk, staggered into some woods and passed out, but something happened that changed my life for eternity. As I look back, I see some simple steps that I took that brought real change to my life.

Number One: I got fed up! Someone so accurately said, "When the pain of staying the same becomes greater than the pain of change, you will change!"

I got fed up with my life, looking at a loser in the mirror every morning. Until you get mad, nothing much will happen. Dr. Mike Murdock says, "What you can tolerate you will never change."

Everything that I had tried had not worked, my way failed miserably. That led to step Number Two: I looked up! It wasn't until I looked up that anything changed. As long as I looked to Sherman, I failed. When I couldn't stand the pain anymore, I looked up and said, "Jesus, I mean business, help me."

I believe it's a big day in your life when you finally say, "Lord, I can't do it."

You will hear a big "Amen" from heaven. I believe you have to realize that's why Jesus didn't send you to the cross, because you can't do it, only Jesus can.

After I looked up, I came to step Number Three: I gave up. It wasn't easy, I was used to being in control. I had come to my end; I had to cry, "Uncle, I give, I give!"

I struggled for about six months. After I looked up it wasn't easy to say, "Lord I surrender."

I believe that's why many do not get saved. For six months I prayed, "Lord, save me," but nothing happened, because I wouldn't let go.

I talked to a man recently who was under conviction. He told me he was suffering. I asked him why didn't he receive the Lord. He replied, "I'm not ready."

I thought you just have to suffer a little more, you aren't hurting enough. Understand, it's not natural to give up, we are survivors by nature. If you don't let the old man die, you will never walk in the power of the new man. Our problem many times is that we want the Resurrection life without first dying. Jesus said that unless a grain of wheat falls to the ground, it remains alone. I was alone! Me and my old man. Then in the next verse Jesus says, "he who loves his life will lose it."

I fell to the ground and died. The rich young ruler wouldn't give up, and he lost it all. So I got fed up, I looked up, then I gave up, then I got fired up. After a few years I began to lose my fire; then I was introduced to the Holy Spirit. The early church was baptized with the Holy Spirit and fire. A few years later I developed a hunger for God's Word. The Holy Spirit and the Word of God give you power for living. After I was fired up, I showed up. For what? Everything! I helped in the bus ministry, children's ministry, and anywhere I could help. I would do anything I was asked. I didn't understand this at the time, but involvement surfaces your gift. Tell me and I forget, teach me and I remember, involve me and I learn. As I got busy, I began to see my gift to teach come to the surface.

I tell young ministers, Get Busy! Clean bathrooms, pick up paper, straighten the chairs, give a half a day a week helping with anything that is asked. Don't pray about it, do it! God calls busy people. Dr. Norvel Hayes says, "God can't bless lazy people and stingy people."

It's also important that you show up in one place, not all over town. You will never grow until you are planted.

After I showed up, I began to grow up. I thought I was through with studying when I left school. Little did I know. I began to listen to men like Kenneth Hagin and Kenneth Copeland. I listened to tapes day and night. I kept my Copeland-Hagin with me all the time. I began to renew my mind. Nothing happens until you change your thinking. We used to say this in church a lot, "I don't know what you've been thinkin', but you gotta get rid of that stinkin' thinkin'; if you keep on thinkin' what you've always thought, you'll keep on gettin' what you've always got."

When you are through improving, you are through!

So I got:

(1) Fed up

(2) I looked up

(3) I gave up

(4) I showed up

(5) I grew up

(6) I helped up

I believe it's important that you take someone with you. To be all I can be, I must help you be all you can be.

It has been said, "If you help people with their needs, you will always be needed."

Your door out of trouble is somebody in trouble.

After you begin to help up, don't shut up! Tell everyone what the Lord has done for you.

Lastly, I believe if you take these steps you will Go Up. One word stands out to me in all these steps —Obedience. You stumble over happiness on the road of obedience.

Don Shelby says, "When we tell ourselves 'I can never change' or that 'It will never happen,' we presume too much and believe too little."

Amen and Amen!

The Rewards Of The Future Are For Those Who Are Willing To Change.

Your Letter Is Very Important To Me

My dear friend,
I believe in the power of God, the power of prayer, and the power of agreement. If you are facing spiritual needs or conflict in your life, write me. I will pray and agree with you for breakthrough. If you have any questions concerning this book, I will do my best to answer them. Keep aiming high and I will see you at the top in Christ!

Sherman Owens

For additional information about Pastor Sherman ministering at your church or group, or for additional copies of "Why Don't They Teach This In Bible School?" write the author at:

Sherman Owens
8200 Bee Ridge Rd.
Sarasota, FL 34241

CASSETTE TAPE ORDER FORM

Name Of Item	Quantity	Price	Total
Why Don't They Teach This In Bible School? (Book)		$8.95	
The Ladder To The Top (4 Tapes)		$20.00	
Marriage (7 Tapes)		$35.00	
Joseph's Three Coats (4 Tapes)		$20.00	
The Seven F's Of Faith (3 Tapes)		$15.00	
Seven Old Men (3 Tapes)		$15.00	
God's Strategy For Success (5 Tapes)		$25.00	
Six Qualities Of A Super Achiever (2 Tapes)		$10.00	
How To Get Through What You're Going Through (8 Tapes)		$40.00	
Why Bad Things Happen To Good People (2 Tapes)		$10.00	
Transference Of Spirits (2 Tapes)		$10.00	
Family (4 Tapes)		$20.00	
Power Pack For Achievers (6 Tapes)		$30.00	
The Law Of The Farm (2 Tapes)		$10.00	
		Add 10% For Shipping	
		TOTAL AMOUNT ENCLOSED	

Please Print

Name ____

Address ____

City ____

State ____________________ Zip ____________________

☐ Check ☐ Money Order ☐ Cash ☐ VISA ☐ Mastercard

Signature ______________________________

Card # _________________________________

Expiration Date _________________________

Mail to:

Victory Christian Family Center

8200 Bee Ridge Road Sarasota, Florida 34241